# The GREATEST POP Hits OF 1997-1998

**Arranged by**
Dan Coates &
John Brimhall

MW00681804

Project Manager: Carol Cuellar
Art Design: Lisa Greene Mane

# CONTENTS

# MMMBOP

Arranged by
*JOHN BRIMHALL*

Words and Music by
ISAAC HANSON, TAYLOR HANSON
and ZAC HANSON

Mmmbop - 6 - 1

© 1997 JAM 'N' BREAD MUSIC (ASCAP)
All Rights Reserved

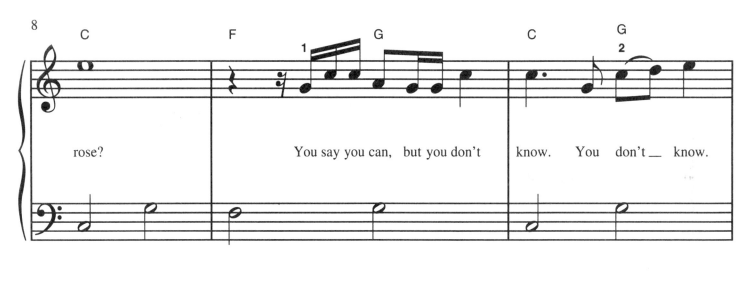

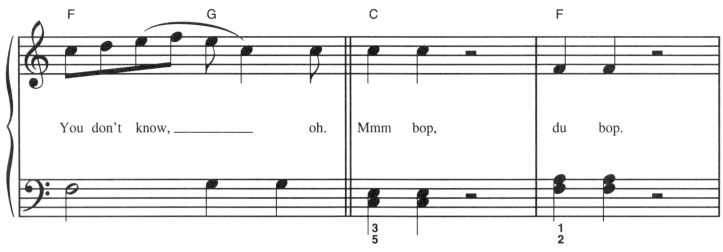

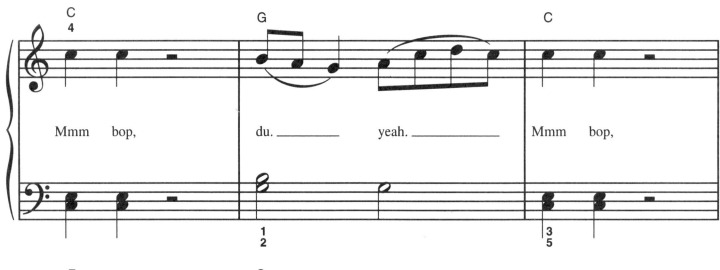

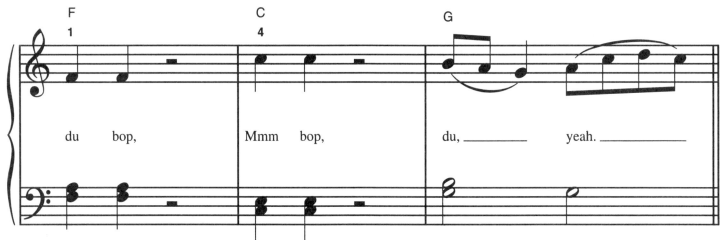

*Repeat ad lib. and fade*

*Verse 2:*
So hold on to the ones who really care,
In the end, they'll be the only one there.
When you get old and start losing your hair,
Can you tell me who will still care?
Can you tell me who will still care?
Oh, oh, care.

*Verse 3:*
Plant a seed, plant a flower, plant a rose.
You can plant any one of those.
Keep planting to find out which one grows.
It's a secret no one knows.
It's a secret no one knows.
Oh, no one knows.

# QUIT PLAYING GAMES
## (With My Heart)

Words and Music by
MAX MARTIN and HERBERT CRICHLOW
*Arranged by DAN COATES*

**Bright rock tempo**

heart, _____ with my heart, my heart.

I should have known from the start. My heart, my

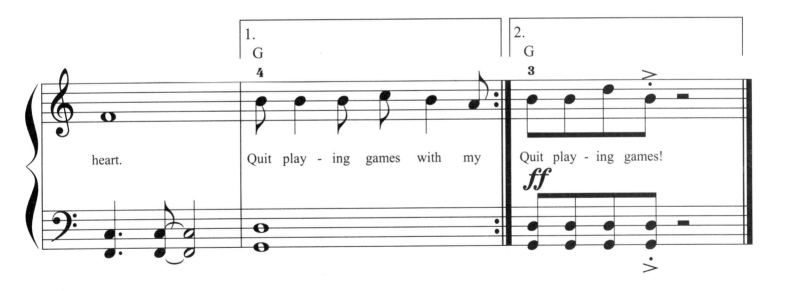

heart. Quit play - ing games with my Quit play - ing games!

*Verse 2:*
I live my life the way,
To keep you comin' back to me.
Everything I do is for you,
So what is it that you can't see?
Sometimes I wish that I could turn back time,
Impossible as it may seem.
But I wish I could so bad, baby,
Quit playing games with my heart.

# SAY YOU'LL BE THERE

*Arranged by*
*JOHN BRIMHALL*

Words and Music by
**SPICE GIRLS** and
**ELIOT KENNEDY**

Oh, say you'll be there giv-ing you eve - ry - thing,_ all that

joy can bring,_ this I swear._ 1. Last time

that we had this con-ver-sa-tion I de-ci-ded we should be friends,_ yeah.

Say You'll Be There - 4 - 1

16

fool can see ___ they're fall - ing, I got - ta make you un - der -

stand. _____ (I'll) I'm giv - ing you eve - ry - thing, _ all that

joy can bring, _ this I swear. _ And all that I

want from you ___ is a prom - ise you ___ will be there, say you will be

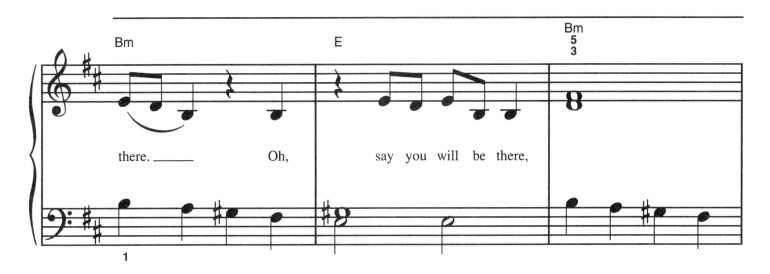

*Verse 2:*
If you put two and two together you will see what our friendship is for,
If you can't work this equation then I guess I'll have to show you the door,
There is no need to say you love me it would be better left unsaid.

I'm giving you everything all that joy can bring this I swear,
And all that I want from you is a promise you will be there,
Yeah I want you.

*Verse 3: (Instrumental)*
Any fool can see they're falling, gotta make you understand.
*(To Chorus:)*

# BUTTERFLY KISSES

Words and Music by
BOB CARLISLE and RANDY THOMAS
*Arranged by DAN COATES*

**Slowly and tenderly**

Butterfly Kisses - 6 - 1

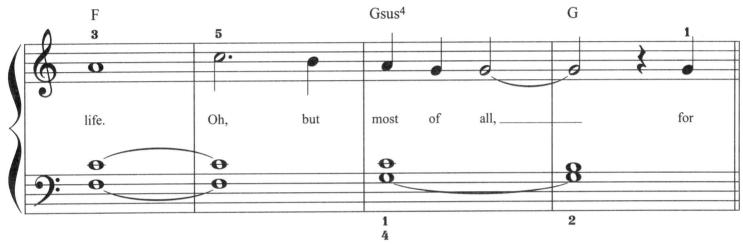

*Chorus:*

Butterfly Kisses - 6 - 2

20

Butterfly Kisses - 6 - 3

22

*Verse 2:*
Sweet sixteen today,
She's lookin' like her mama a little more every day.
One part woman, the other part girl;
To perfume and make-up from ribbons and curls.
Trying her wings out in a great big world.
 But I remember:

*Chorus 2:*
Butterfly kisses after bedtime prayer,
Stickin' little white flowers all up in her hair.
"You know how much I love you, daddy,
But if you don't mind,
I'm only gonna kiss you on the cheek this time."
Oh, with all that I've done wrong,
 I must have done something right
To deserve her love every morning
And butterfly kisses at night.

*Verse 3:*
She'll change her name today.
She'll make a promise, and I'll give her away.
Standing in the bride room just staring at her,
She asks me what I'm thinking, and I say, "I'm not sure.
I just feel like I'm losing my baby girl."
Then she leaned over and gave me...

*Chorus 3:*
Butterfly kisses with her mama there,
Stickin' little white flowers all up in her hair.
"Walk me down the aisle, daddy, it's just about time."
"Does my wedding gown look pretty, daddy?
 Daddy, don't cry."
Oh, with all that I've done wrong,
 I must have done womething right
To deserve her love every morning
And butterfly kisses.   *(Coda)*

Butterfly Kisses - 6 - 6

# AS LONG AS YOU LOVE ME

*Arranged by*
*JOHN BRIMHALL*

By MAX MARTIN

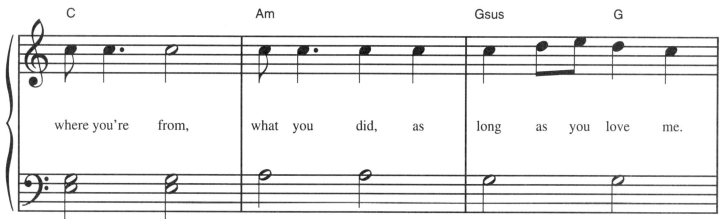

As Long As You Love Me - 4 - 2

26

As Long As You Love Me - 4 - 3

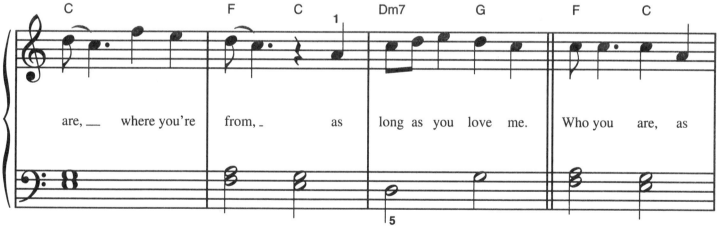

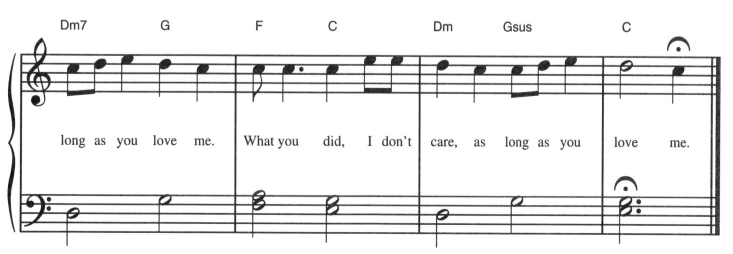

As Long As You Love Me - 4 - 4

*From the Twentieth Century Fox Motion Picture*
*"ANASTASIA"*

# AT THE BEGINNING

Lyrics by
LYNN AHERNS

Music by
STEPHEN FLAHERTY
*Arranged by DAN COATES*

At the Beginning - 5 - 1

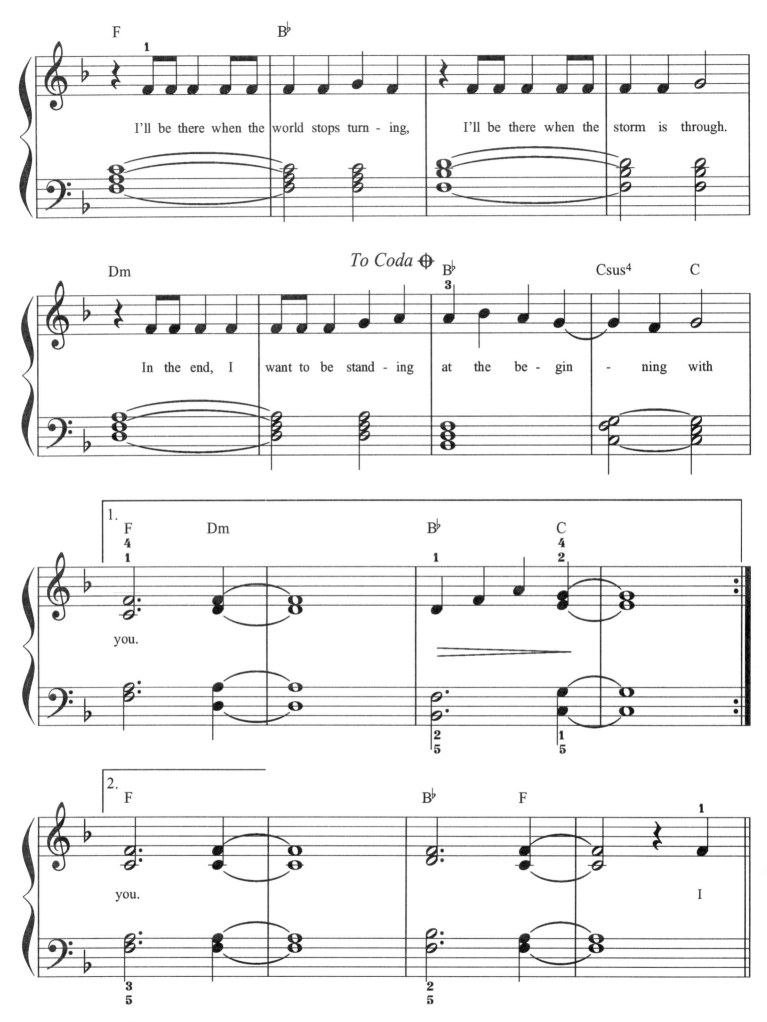

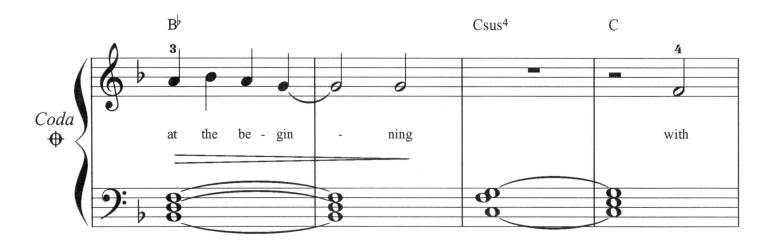

*Coda*

at the be - gin - ning          with

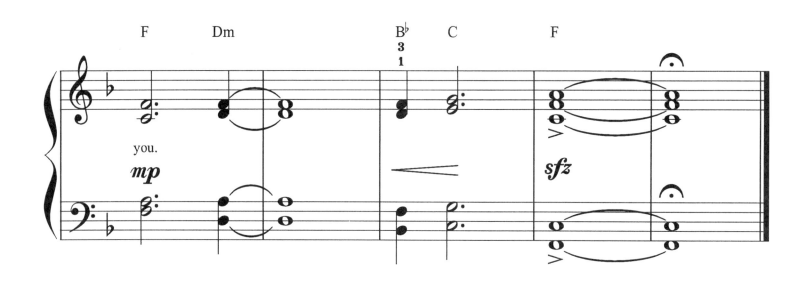

you.
*mp*          *sfz*

*Verse 3:*
We were strangers
On a crazy adventure,
Never dreaming
How our dream would come true.
Now here we stand
Unafraid of the future,
At the beginning with you.
*(To Chorus:)*

# THE DIFFERENCE

Arranged by
*JOHN BRIMHALL*

Words and Music by
JAKOB DYLAN

The Difference - 3 - 1

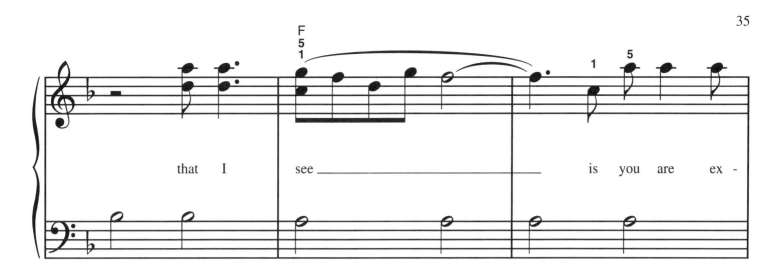

that I see _____ is you are ex-

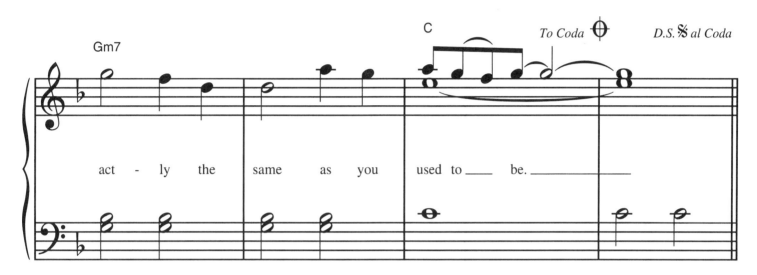

act - ly the same as you used to ___ be. _____

*Verse 2:*
One boy
Lives in a tower
With bow and arrow
And the artificial heart.
With his girl,
The maid of dishonor,
They loaded the cannon
With a jealous appetite.

*Pre-Chorus 2:*
They say that children
Now, they come in all ages.
Then maybe sometimes old men die
With little boy faces.
*(To Chorus:)*

*Pre-Chorus 3:*
You always said that you needed some,
But you always had more, more than anyone.
*(To Chorus:)*

# FOOLISH GAMES

Words and Music by
JEWEL KILCHER
*Arranged by DAN COATES*

38

*Verse 2:*
You're always the mysterious one
With dark eyes and careless hair,
You were fashionably sensitive
But too cool to care.
You stood in my doorway with nothing to say
Besides some comment on the weather.
*(To Bridge:)*

*Verse 3:*
You're always brilliant in the morning,
Smoking your cigarettes and talking over coffee.
Your philosophies on art, Baroque moved you.
You loved Mozart and you'd speak of your loved ones
As I clumsily strummed my guitar.

*Verse 4:*
You'd teach me of honest things,
Things that were daring, things that were clean.
Things that knew what an honest dollar did mean.
I hid my soiled hands behind my back.
Somehwere along the line,
I must have gone off track with you.

*Bridge 2:*
Excuse me, I think I've mistaken you
For somebody else, somebody who gave a damn,
Somebody more like myself.
*(To Chorus:)*

Foolish Games - 4 - 4

*From the Twentieth Century-Fox Motion Picture "ONE FINE DAY"*

# FOR THE FIRST TIME

*Arranged by*
*JOHN BRIMHALL*

Words and Music by
JAMES NEWTON HOWARD,
ALLAN RICH and JUD FRIEDMAN

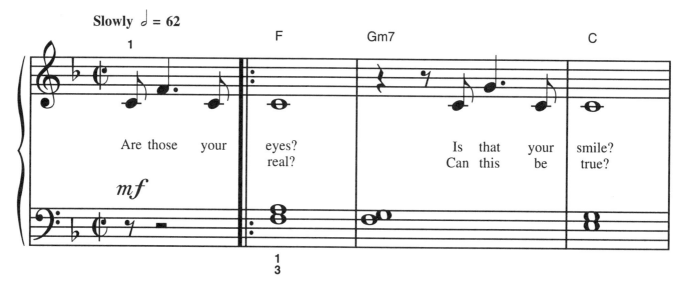

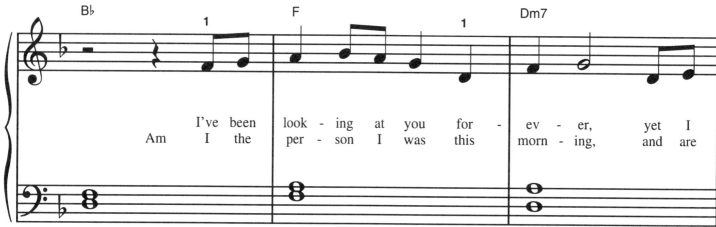

For the First Time - 4 - 1

42

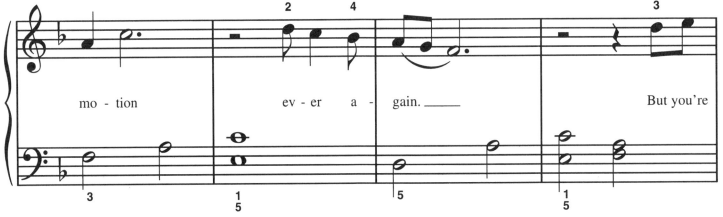

# FOR YOU I WILL

Arranged by
*JOHN BRIMHALL*

Words and Music by
DIANE WARREN

# FOUR LEAF CLOVER

*Arranged by*
*JOHN BRIMHALL*

Words and Music by
**ABRA MOORE**

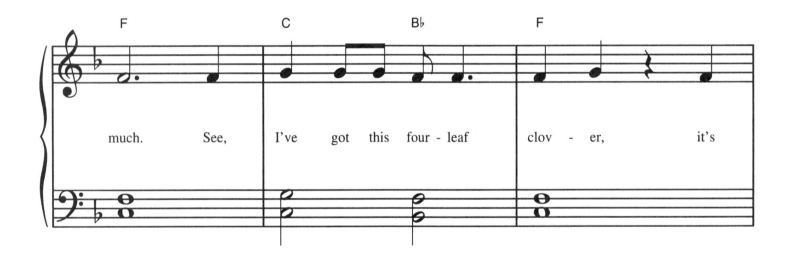

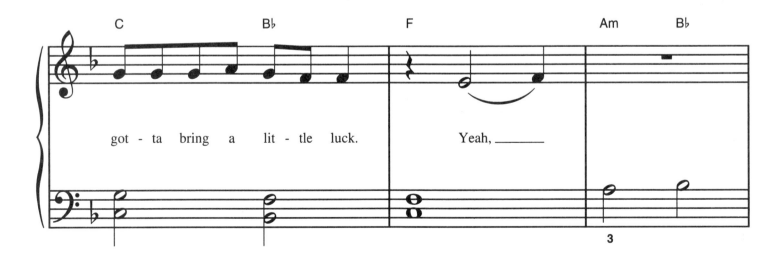

Four Leaf Clover - 4 - 1

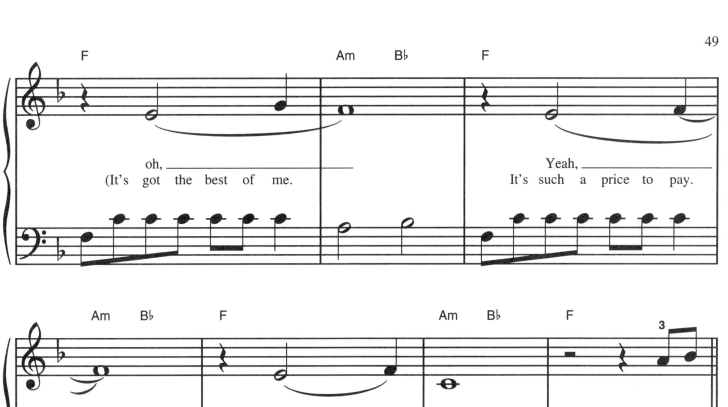

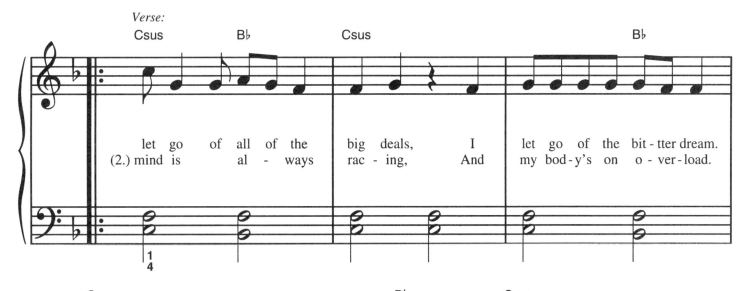

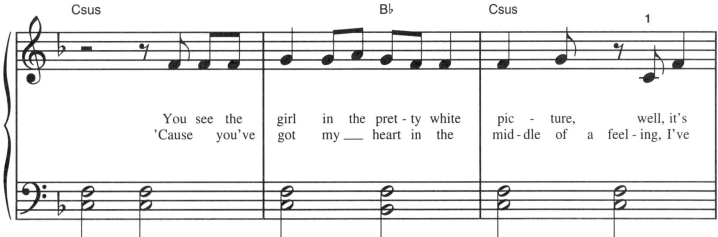

Four Leaf Clover - 4 - 2

Four Leaf Clover - 4 - 4

# FROM HERE TO ETERNITY

*Arranged by*
*JOHN BRIMHALL*

Words and Music by
MICHAEL PETERSON and
ROBERT ELLIS ORRALL

54

*Verse 2:*
Well, I saved a year for this ring,
I can't wait to see how it looks on your hand.
I'll give you everything that one woman needs
From a one-woman man.
I'll be strong, I'll be tender, a man of my word.
And I will be yours...
*(To Chorus:)*

# KISS THE RAIN

Words and Music by
ERIC BAZILIAN, DESMOND CHILD
and BILLIE MYERS
*Arranged by DAN COATES*

**Moderately slow**

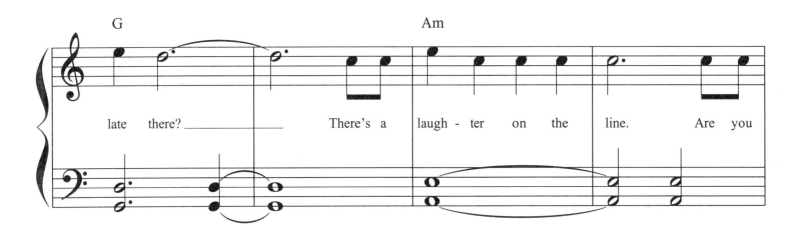

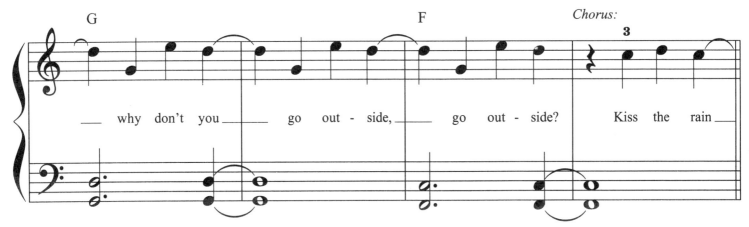

Kiss the Rain - 5 - 3

*Verse 2:*
Hello?  Do you miss me?
I hear you say you do,
But not the way I'm missing you.
What's new?  How's the weather?
Is it stormy where you are?
You sound so close,
But it feels like you're so far.
Oh, would it mean anything
If you knew what I'm left imagining
In my mind, in my mind.
Would you go, would go...
*(To Chorus:)*

# GOTHAM CITY

Arranged by
*JOHN BRIMHALL*

Words and Music by
R. KELLY

**Slowly** ♩ = 92

*Bridge:*

# HOW DO I LIVE

Words and Music by
DIANE WARREN
*Arranged by DAN COATE*

**Moderately slow**

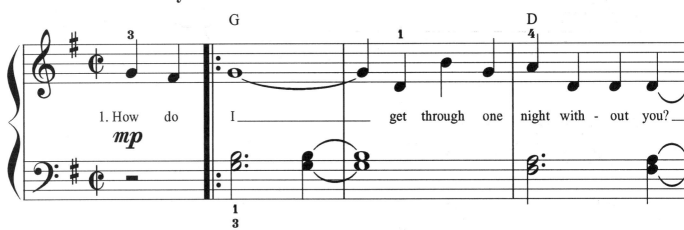

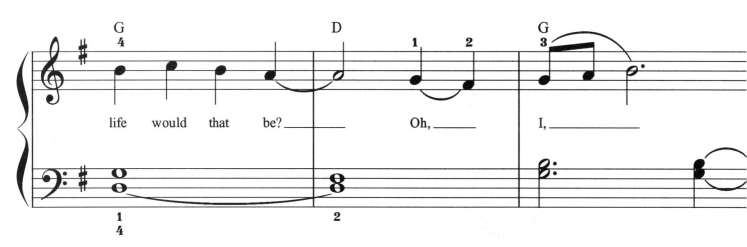

How Do I Live - 4 - 1

66

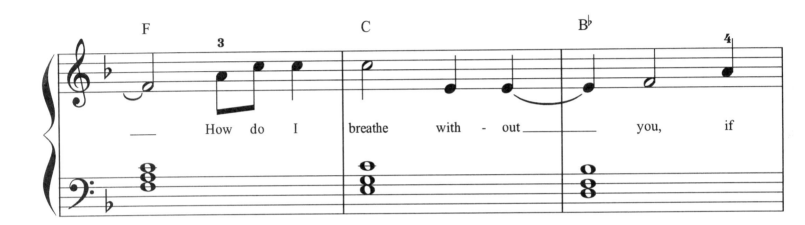

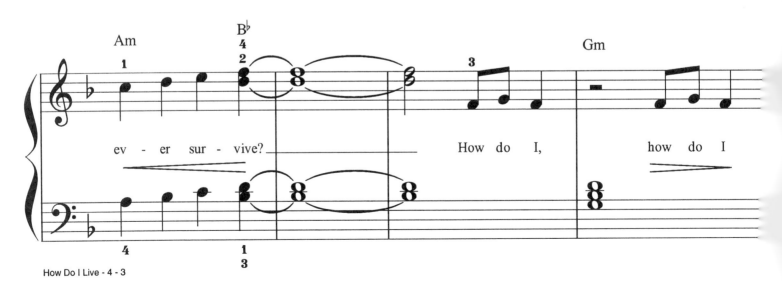

How Do I Live - 4 - 3

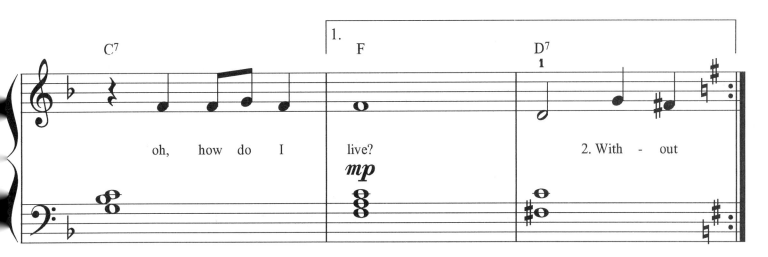

oh, how do I live?
*mp*
2. With - out

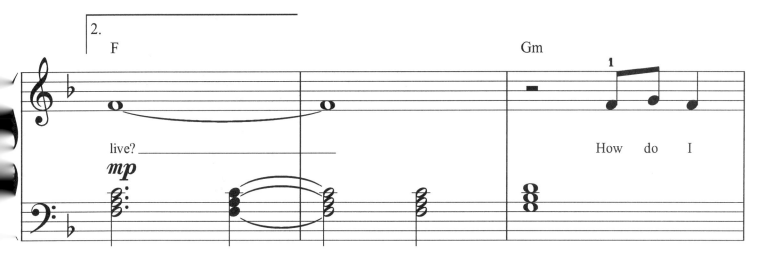

live? _____
*mp*
How do I

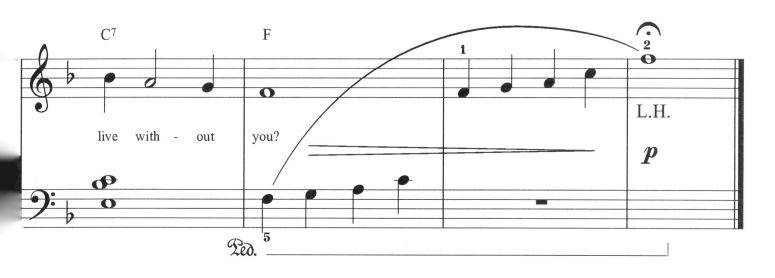

live with - out you?
L.H.
*p*

*Verse 2:*
Without you, there'd be no sun up in my sky,
There would be no love in my life,
There'd be no world left for me.
And I, baby, I don't know what I would do,
I'd be lost if I lost you.
If you ever leave,
Baby, you would take away everything
Real in my life.
And tell me now...
*(To Chorus:)*

# I'M NOT GIVING YOU UP

Arranged by
*JOHN BRIMHALL*

Words by
GLORIA ESTEFAN
Music by
KIKE SANTANDER

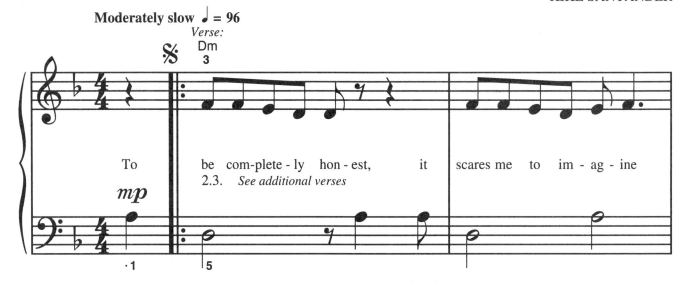

To be com-plete-ly hon-est, it scares me to im-ag-ine
2.3. *See additional verses*

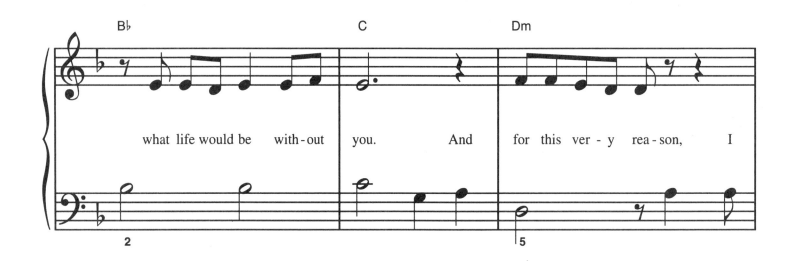

what life would be with-out you. And for this ver-y rea-son, I

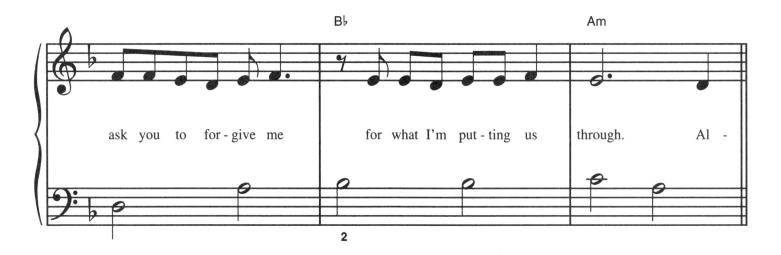

ask you to for-give me for what I'm put-ting us through. Al-

I'm Not Giving You Up - 4 - 1

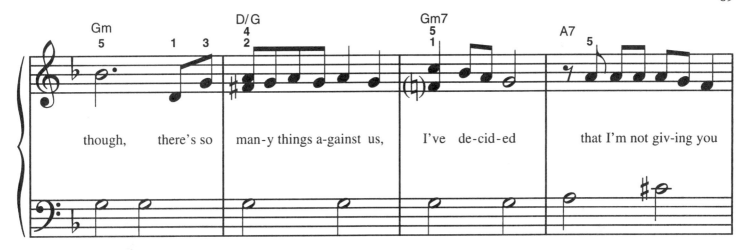

though, there's so | man-y things a-gainst us, | I've de-cid-ed | that I'm not giv-ing you

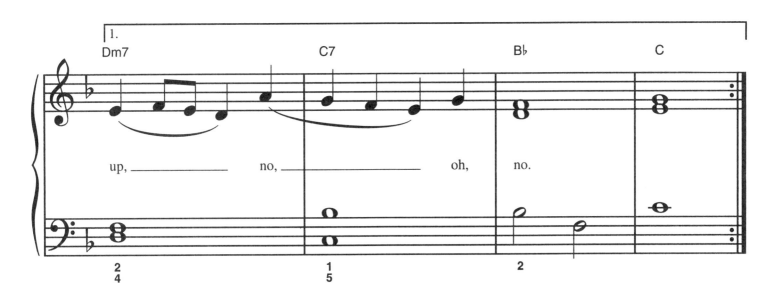

up, _____ no, _____ oh, no.

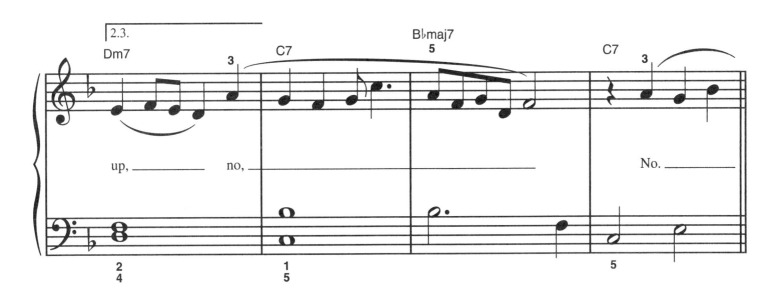

up, _____ no, _____ No. _____

I'm Not Giving You Up - 4 - 2

D.S. 𝄋 al Coda

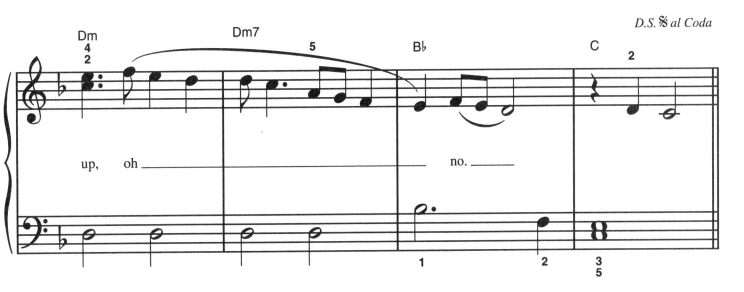

up, oh _____ no. _____

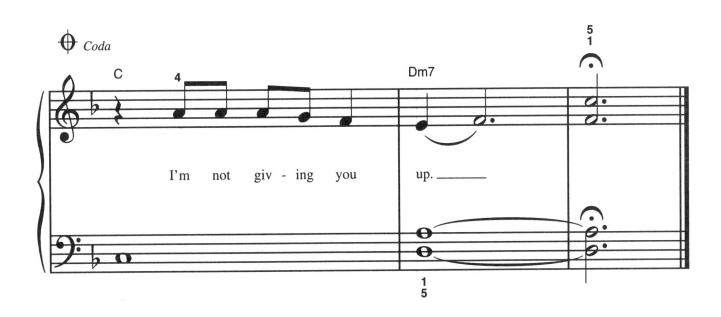

I'm not giv - ing you up. _____

*Verse 2:*
Thinking back, I see what we have is something different,
I think we've known all along.
So how fair would it be to divide this love's existence
Between what's right and what's wrong.
And you, always wond'ring if we'll make it.
Time will tell you that I'm not giving you up, oh no.

*Verse 3:*
Screaming in the silence, the promises we've spoken
Come back to haunt me false and broken.
Quiet desperation to see we're lost forever,
Searching for water in the desert.
No, I refuse to have to do without your kisses.
I'm not giving you up, no.

# I SAY A LITTLE PRAYER

Words by
HAL DAVID

Music by
BURT BACHARACH
*Arranged by DAN COATES*

**Brightly**

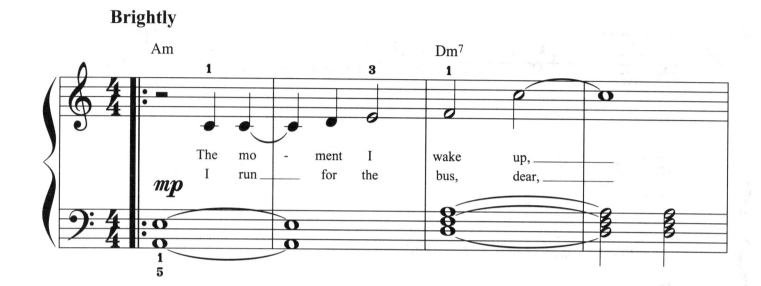

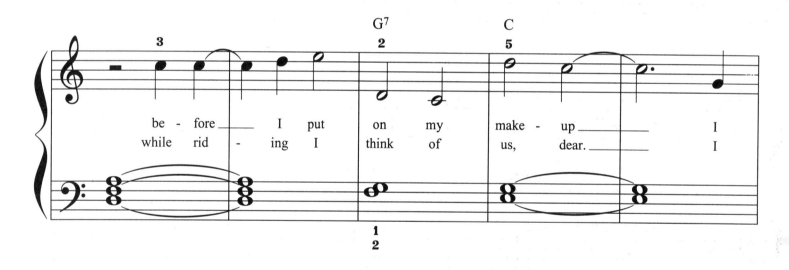

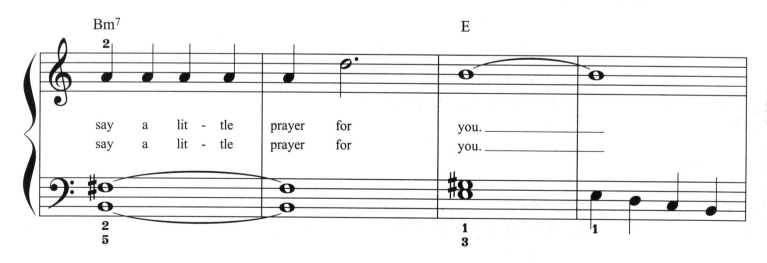

I Say a Little Prayer - 4 - 1

# I WILL COME TO YOU

Words and Music by
ISAAC HANSON, TAYLOR HANSON, ZACHARY HANSON,
BARRY MANN and CYNTHIA WEIL
*Arranged by DAN COATES*

**Moderately slow**

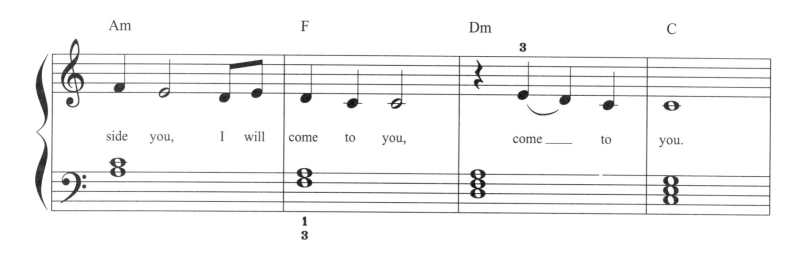

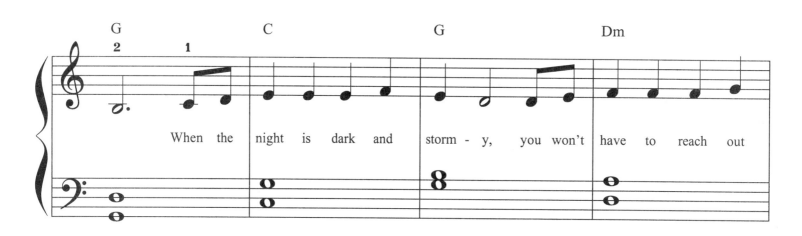

I Will Come to You - 4 - 1

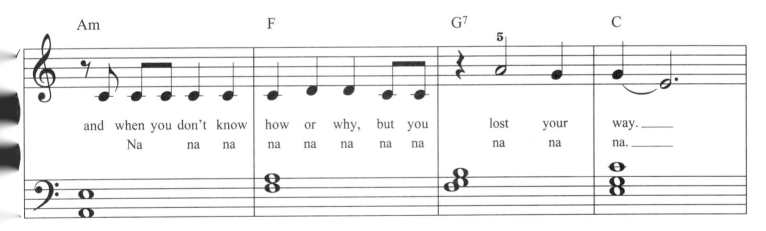

Will Come to You - 4 - 2

78

I Will Come to You - 4 - 3

# IN ANOTHER'S EYES

*Arranged by*
*JOHN BRIMHALL*

Words and Music by
BOBBY WOOD, JOHN PEPPARD
and GARTH BROOKS

**Slowly** ♩ = 72

*Verses 1 & 2:*

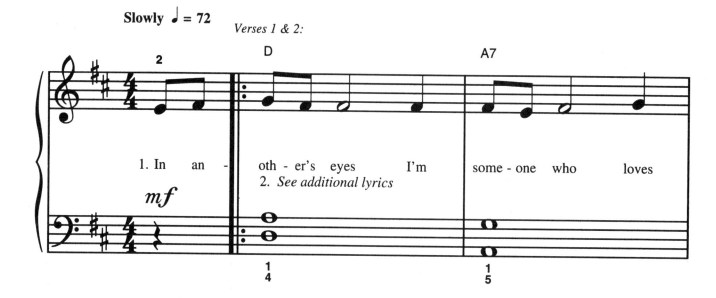

In Another's Eyes - 4 - 1

82

*Verse 2:*
In another's eyes, I can do no wrong.
He believes in me and his faith is strong.
I'd never fall or even compromise,
In another's eyes.
*(To Chorus:)*

# MY HEART WILL GO ON

Words and Music by
JAMES HORNER and WILL JENNINGS
*Arranged by DAN COATES*

**Slow ballad**

# RETURN OF THE MACK

Words and Music by
PHIL CHILL and MARK MORRISON

Return of the Mack - 3 - 1

88

Return of the Mack - 3 - 2

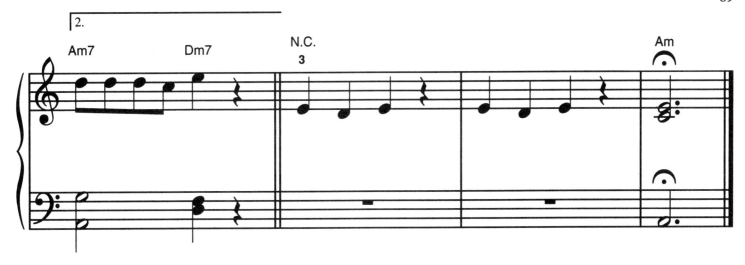

*Verse 2:*
So I'm back in the game
Running things to keep my swing
Letting all the people know
That I'm back to run the show
Cos what you did you know was wrong
And all the nasty things you've done
So baby listen carefully
While I sing my comeback song.

You lied to me
Cos she said she'd never turn on me
You lied to me
But you did, but you did
You lied to me
But I do, but I do, do do.

Return of the Mack
    *Here it is*
Return of the Mack
    *Hold on*
Return of the Mack
    *Don't you know*
Return of the Mack
    *Here I go*
Return of the Mack
    *Oh little girl*
Return of the Mack
    *Wants my pearl*
Return of the Mack
    *Up and down*
You know that I'll be back
    *Round and round.*

*D. %*
You lied to me
Cos she said she'd never turn on me
You lied to me
But you did, but you did
You lied to me
All these things you said I'd never do
You lied to me
But I do, but I do, do, do.

# SAND AND WATER

*Arranged by*
*JOHN BRIMHALL*

Words and Music by
BETH NIELSEN CHAPMAN

**Moderately** ♩ = 112

*Verse:*

1. All a - lone, I _____ did - n't

like the feel - ing. _____ All a - lone, I _____ sat and cried. _

All a - lone, I _____ had to

find some mean - ing ___ in the cen - ter of the pain I felt ___ in -

Sand and Water - 3 - 1

Sand and Water - 3 - 2

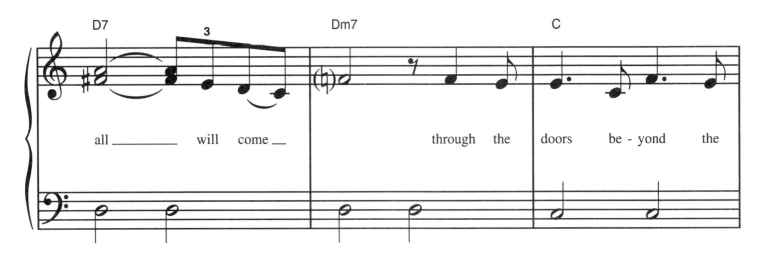

all _____ will come ___ through the doors be - yond the

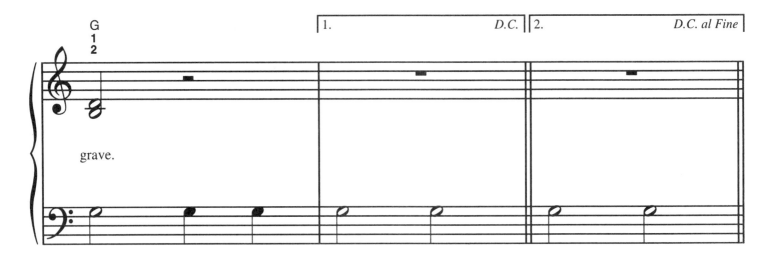

grave.

*Verses 2 & 4:*
All alone I came into this world,
All alone I will someday die.
Solid stone is just sand and water, baby,
Sand and water and a million years gone by.
*(To Chorus/Coda:)*

*Verse 3:*
All alone I heal this heart of sorrow,
All alone I raise this child.
Flesh and bone, he's just bursting towards tomorrow,
And his laughter fills my world and wears your smile.
*(To Chorus:)*

# SOMETHING ABOUT THE WAY YOU LOOK TONIGHT

Lyrics by
BERNIE TAUPIN

Music by
ELTON JOHN
*Arranged by DAN COATES*

96

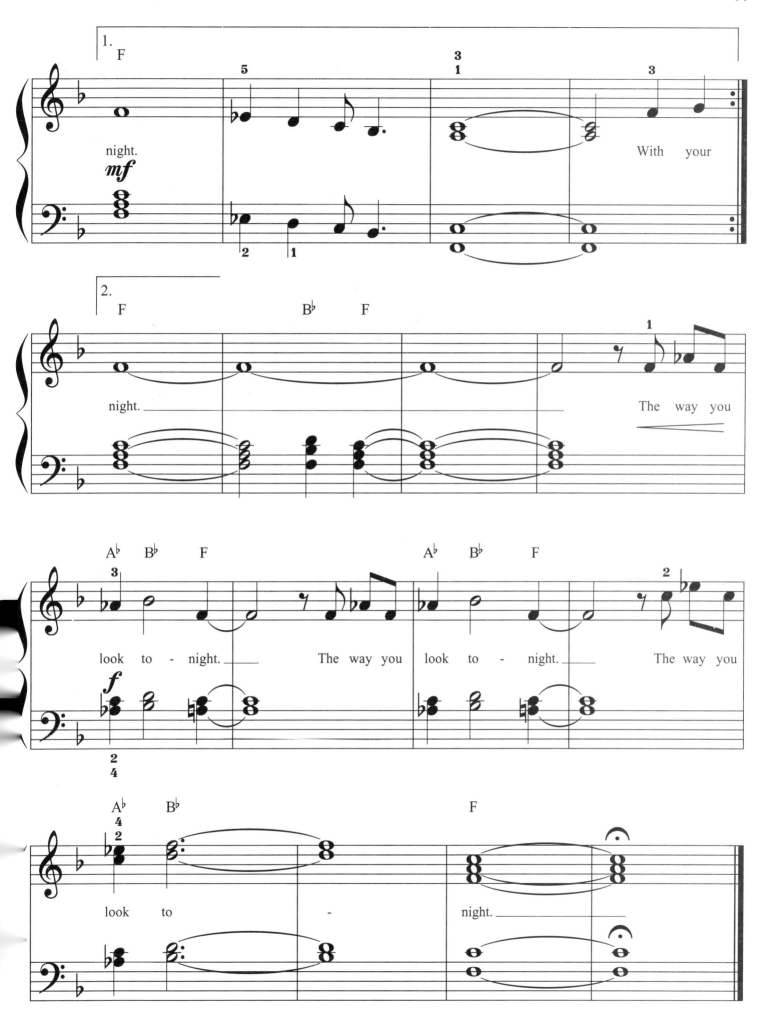

# SO HELP ME GIRL

*Arranged by*
*JOHN BRIMHALL*

Words and Music by
HOWARD PERDEW
and ANDY SPOONER

So Help Me Girl - 4 - 1

ev - 'ry dream I've ev - er had. _____ So help me

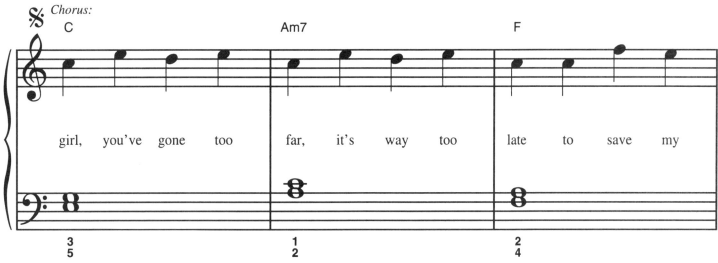

*Chorus:*

girl, you've gone too far, it's way too late to save my

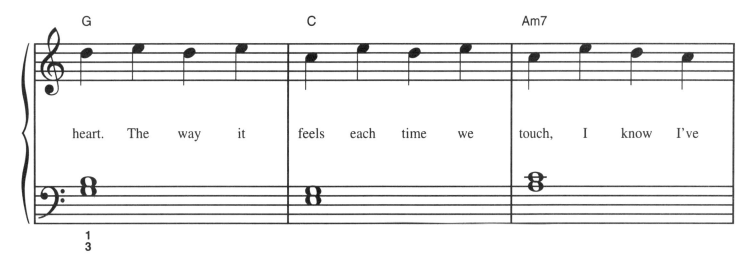

heart. The way it feels each time we touch, I know I've

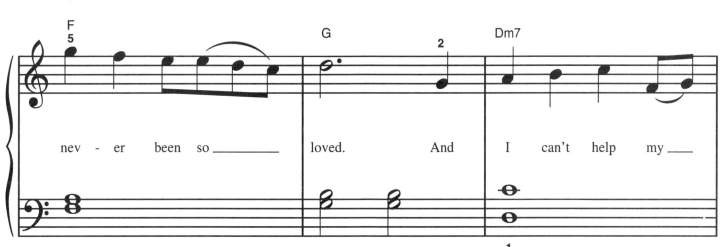

nev - er been so _____ loved. And I can't help my ___

Fall - in', fall - in', fall - in', you've got me fall - in', Fall - in', fall - in',

*Repeat ad lib. and fade*

Fall - in', fall - in', fall - in', fall - in', fall - in', You've got me fall - in'.

*Verse 2:*
You had to be there until the song came on,
Makin' last night feel like a vision of things yet to come.
You just start to hold me like nobody else.
Look what you've gone and done.
You had to love me till I just can't get enough.
*(To Chorus:)*

# SOMETHING THAT WE DO

*Arranged by*
*JOHN BRIMHALL*

Words and Music by
CLINT BLACK and SKIP EWING

Something That We Do - 5 - 1

*Verse 3:*

a tempo

Am7 | D | G | D/G
end and where — you start. It gives me heart, — re- mem-b'ring how — we —

C | G | C
— start - ed with a sim - ple vow. — There's — so much to — look

G | Am7 | D | G
back on now. — Still it feels — brand new. We're on a road — that

D/G | C | G
has no end, — and each day we be- gin a - gain. — Love's

C | G | Am | D7sus | G *D.S. % al Coda*
not just some - thing that we're in, it's some-thing that — we do.

Verse 2:
It's holding tight, lettin' go,
It's flyin' high and layin' low.
Let your strongest feelings show
And your weakness, too.
It's a little and a lot to ask,
An endless and a welcome task.
Love isn't something that we have,
It's something that we do.
(To Bridge:)

# A SONG FOR MAMA

Arranged by
*JOHN BRIMHALL*

Words and Music by
KENNETH "BABYFACE" EDMONDS

**Slowly** ♩ = 76
*Verse:*

1. You taught me ev - 'ry - thing and ev - 'ry - thing you've giv - en me,
2. *See additional lyrics*

I al-ways keep it in - side.

You're the driv - ing force in my life.

There is - n't an - y - thing or an - y - one that I could be,

and it just would-n't feel __ right

if I did-n't have __ you by my

A Song for Mama - 5 - 1

108

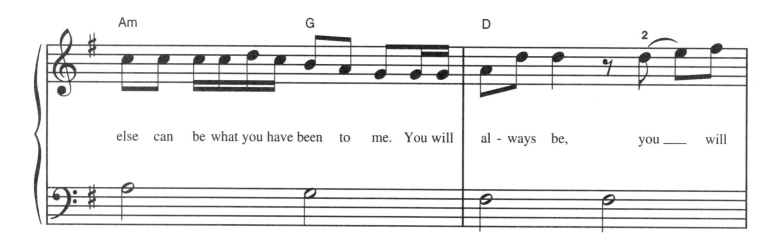

A Song for Mama - 5 - 2

soul. _____

You are the food _____ to my soul.

*Verse 2:*
You're always down for me, have always been around for me,
Even when I was bad.
You'd show me the right from the wrong,
You always did understand.
You gave me strength to go on,
There were so many times, looking back, when I was so afraid.
And then you'd come to me and say I could face anything.
And no one else could do what you have done for me.
You will always be, you will always be
The girl in my life for all times.

# SPICE UP YOUR LIFE

*Arranged by*
*JOHN BRIMHALL*

Words and Music by
SPICE GIRLS, MATT ROWE
and RICHARD STANNARD

Spice up Your Life - 4 - 1

114

Spice up Your Life - 4 - 3

# STAR WARS
## (Main Theme)

Music by
JOHN WILLIAMS
*Arranged by DAN COATES*

Star Wars - 3 - 1

118

# TELL HIM

Words and Music by
LINDA THOMPSON, DAVID FOSTER
and WALTER AFANASIEFF
*Arranged by DAN COATES*

**Slowly**

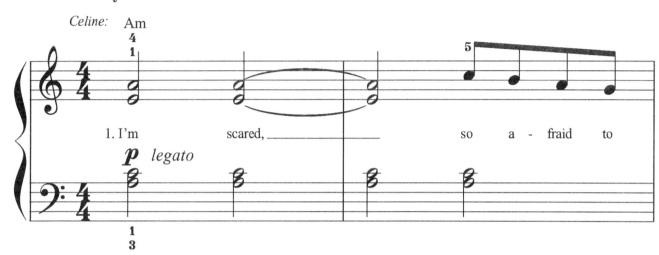

*Celine:*

1. I'm scared, _____ so a-fraid to

show I care. _____ Will he think me weak

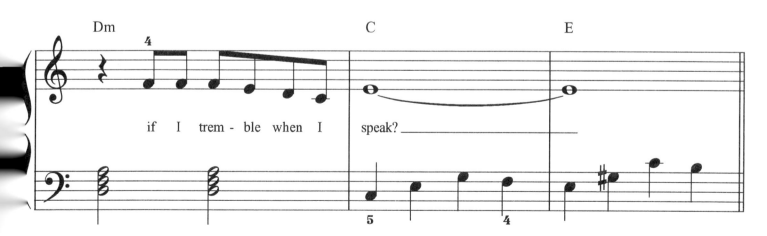

if I trem - ble when I speak? _____

Tell Him - 5 - 1

122

Tell Him - 5 - 4

D.S. 𝄋 al Coda

faith will lead love where it has to go.

*Coda*

Love will be the gift you give your - self.

Nev - er let him go.

*mp* *rit.*

*Verse 2:*
*(Barbra:)*
Touch him with the gentleness you feel inside.
Your love can't be denied.
The truth will set you free.
You'll have what's meant to be.
All in time, you'll see.
*(Celine:)*
I love him,
Of that much I can be sure.
I don't think I could endure
If I let him walk away
When I have so much to say.
*(To Chorus:)*

# SUNNY CAME HOME

*Arranged by*
*JOHN BRIMHALL*

Words and Music by
SHAWN COLVIN and JOHN LEVENTHAL

**Moderately** ♩ = 96

*Verse:*

1. Sun-ny came home to her fa-v'rite room. Sun-ny sat down in the

kitch - en. She o-pened a book and a box of tools.

Sun-ny came home with a mis - sion. She says, "Days go by, I'm

hyp - no - tized. _____ I'm walk-ing on a wire. _____ I

126

# TOGETHER AGAIN

Words and Music by
JANET JACKSON, JAMES HARRIS III,
TERRY LEWIS and RENE ELIZONDO, JR.
*Arranged by DAN COATES*

**Moderately fast**

1. There are times when I look a - bove and be -
2. Al - ways been a true an - gel to me. Now a -

yond, there are times when I feel your love a - round me, ba - by.
bove, I can't wait for you to wrap your wings a - round me, ba - by.

I'll nev - er for - get my ba - by.
Wrap them a - round me, ba - by.

132

*Verse 3:*
There are times when I look above and beyond,
There are times when I feel you smile upon me, baby.
I'll never forget my baby.
What I'd give just to hold you close,
As on earth, in heaven we will be together, baby.
Together again, my baby.   *(To Coda:)*

# TOO LATE, TOO SOON

*Arranged by*
*JOHN BRIMHALL*

Words and Music by
JON SECADA, JAMES HARRIS III
and TERRY LEWIS

Too Late, Too Soon - 3 - 1

*Verse 2:*
I wish I would have known,
I wouldn't have left you all alone.
Temptation led you wrong.
Tell me how long this has been goin' on?
'Cause I thought our love was strong,
But I guess I must be dreamin'.
*(To Chorus:)*

# 2 BECOME 1

*Arranged by*
*JOHN BRIMHALL*

Words and Music by
**SPICE GIRLS, MATTHEW ROWEBOTTOM**
**and RICHARD STANNARD**

1. Can - dle light and soul for - ev - er a dream of you and me to - geth - er.
2. *See additional lyrics*

Say you be - lieve ___ it, say you be - lieve ___ it.

Free your mind of doubt and dan - ger, be for real, don't be a stran - ger.

2 Become 1 - 5 - 1

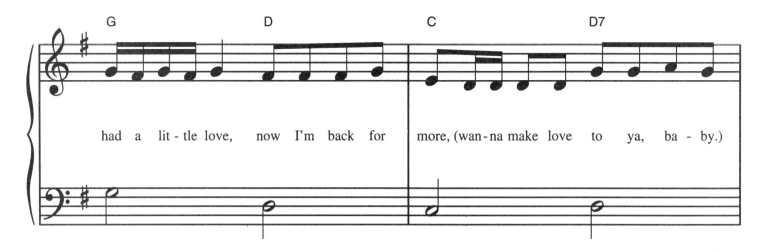

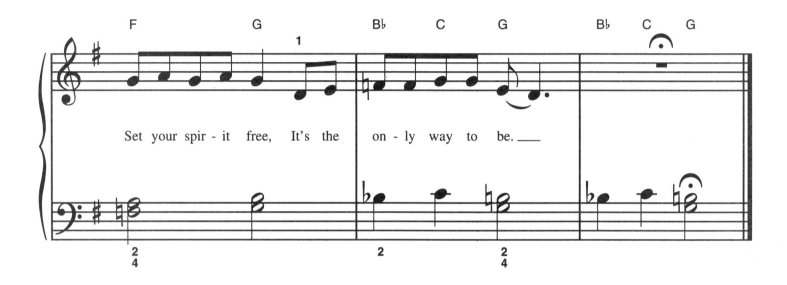

*Verse 2:*
Silly games that you were playing, empty words we both were saying,
Let's work it out, boy, let's work it out, boy.
Any deal that we endeavour, boys and girls feel good together,
Take it or leave it, take it or leave it.
Are you as good as I remember, baby, get it on, get it on,
'Cause tonight is the night when two become one.

I need some love like I never needed love before, (wanna make love to ya, baby.)
I had a little love, now I'm back for more, (wanna make love to ya, baby.)
Set your spirit free, it's the only way to be.

# VALENTINE

Composed by
JIM BRICKMAN and JACK KUGELL
*Arranged by DAN COATES*

Valentine - 3 - 1

*Verse 2:*
All of my life,
I have been waiting for all you give to me.
You've opened my eyes
And shown me how to love unselfishly.
I've dreamed of this a thousand times before,
But in my dreams I couldn't love you more.
I will give you my heart until the end of time.
You're all I need, my love,
My Valentine.

# UNTIL I FIND YOU AGAIN

*Arranged by*
*JOHN BRIMHALL*

Words and Music by
RICHARD MARX

**Moderately slow** ♩ = 76
*Verse:*

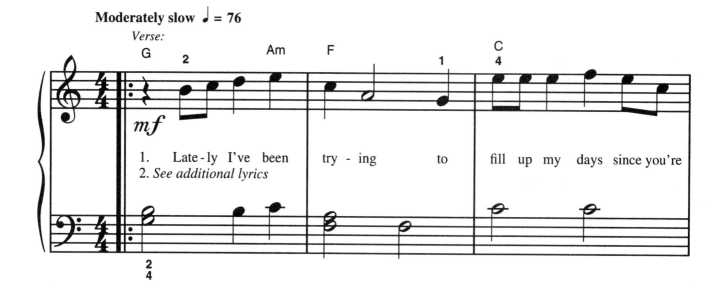

1. Late-ly I've been try - ing to fill up my days since you're
2. *See additional lyrics*

gone. The speed of love is blind - ing and I

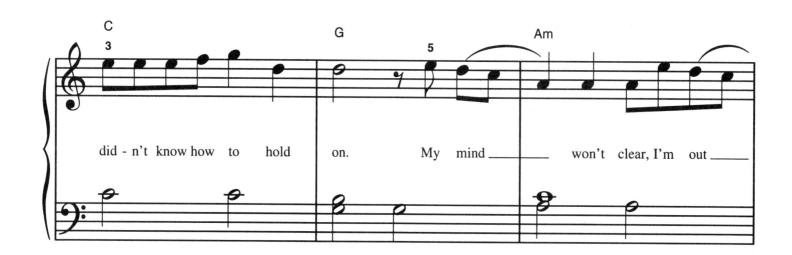

did - n't know how to hold on. My mind_____ won't clear, I'm out_____

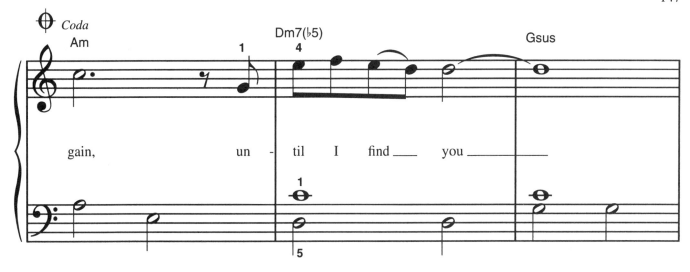

gain, un - til I find ___ you ___

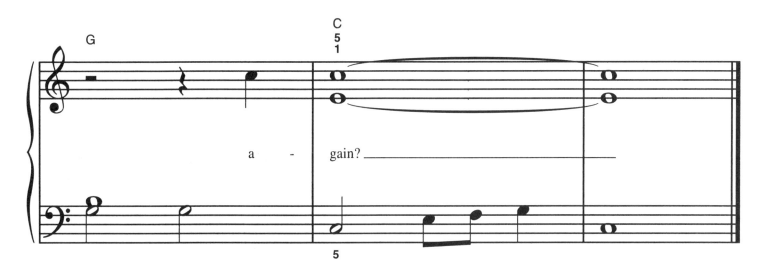

a - gain? ___

*Verse 2:*
Well, the arms of hope surround me.
Will time be a fair-weather friend?
Should I call out to angels
Or just drink myself sober again?
I can't hide the truth, I still burn for you.
Your mem'ry just won't let me go.

# WALKIN' ON THE SUN

Words and Music by
STEVE HARWELL, GREGORY CAMP,
PAUL DeLISLE, and KEVIN COLEMAN
*Arranged by DAN COATES*

**Moderately fast**

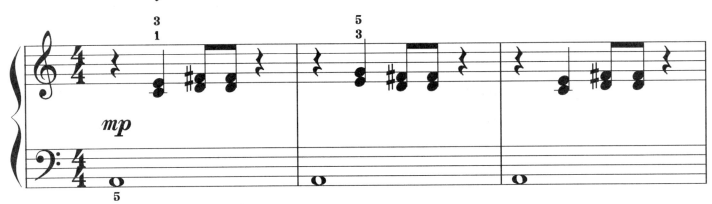

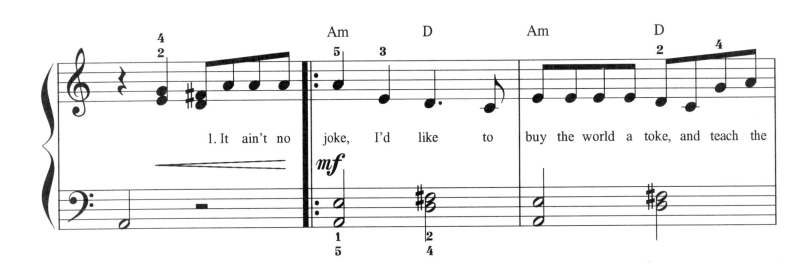

1. It ain't no joke, I'd like to buy the world a toke, and teach the

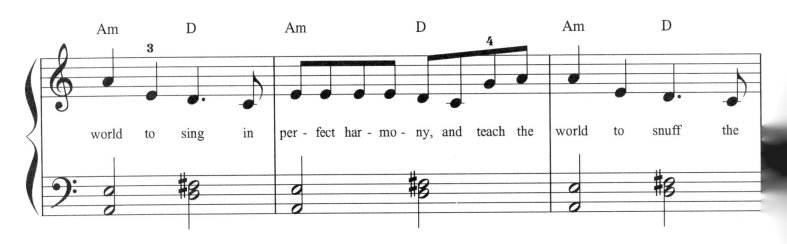

world to sing in per - fect har - mo - ny, and teach the world to snuff the

Walkin' on the Sun - 4 - 1

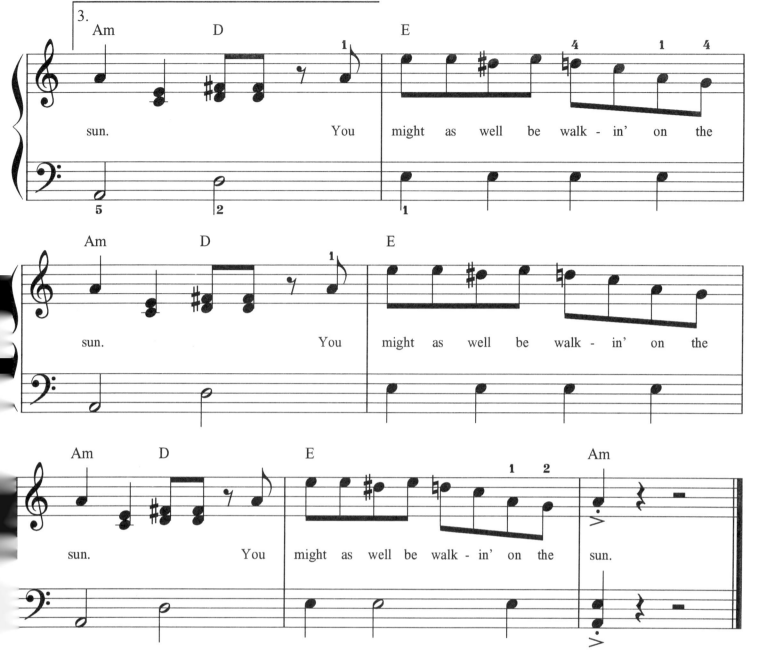

*Verse 2:*
Twenty-five years ago they spoke out
And they broke out of recession and oppression.
And together they toked and they folked out with guitars
Around a bonfire, just singin' and clappin', man, what the hell happened?
Yeah, some were spellbound, some were hell bound,
Some, they fell down and some got back up and fought back against the meltdown.
And their kids were hippie chicks, all hypocrites
Becasue their fashion is smashin' the true meaning of it.
*(To Chorus:)*

*Verse 3:*
It ain't no joke when a mama's handkerchief is soaked
With her tears because her baby's life has been revoked.
The bond is broke up, so choke up and focus on the close-up.
Mister Wizard can perform no god-like hocus pocus.
So don't sit back, kick back and watch the world get bushwacked.
News at ten, your neighborhood is under attack.
Put away the crack before the crack puts you away.
You need to be there when your baby's old enough to relate.
*(To Chorus:)*

# WHAT ABOUT US
## (From "Soul Food")

Words and Music by
MISSY ELLIOTT and TIM MOSLEY

Moderately slow ♩ = 84

*Verse:*

Dm

*mf*

1. Ba - by, I've seen you with an-oth-er la - dy, I just fin-ished hav-ing your
2. *See additional lyrics*

ba - by. Why'd you have to go, _____ go and leave me?

Dm

Ba - by, you know I'm a-bout to be swa - zy. I can't stand my lov - er be - ing

shad - y. Why'd you have to go, _____ go and leave me? _____

Gm7    C

What About Us - 5 - 1

154

What About Us - 5 - 3

1.3.4.   Do do do do do, ____ do do do do do, ____ do do do do do. _
2. *Instrumental solo*

____   1.3. Do do do do do, ____ do do do do do, _

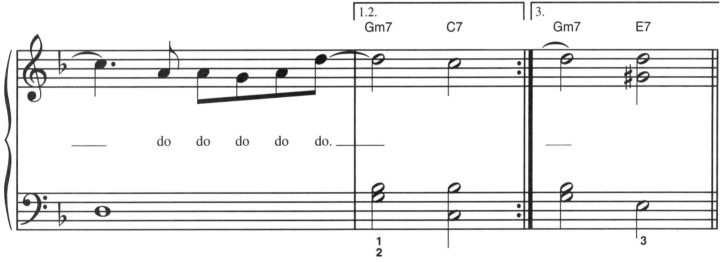

____ do do do do do. ____

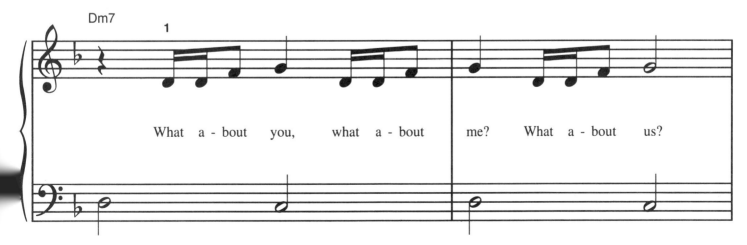

What a-bout you, what a-bout me? What a-bout us?

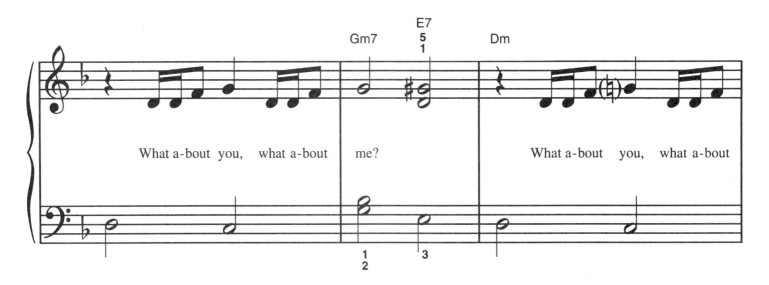

*Verse 2:*
Baby, I know that you've been pimpin'
Mr. Baller, trickin'.
Why'd you have to go, go and leave me?
Baby, I've always been your baby.
Love make a girl go crazy.
I can't understand why you left me.
*(To Chorus:)*

# WHEN I DIE

Arranged by
*JOHN BRIMHALL*

Words and Music by
DIANE WARREN, FRANK FARIAN, DIETMAR KAWOHL
and PETER BISCHOF-FALLENSTEIN

When I Die - 3 - 1

158

When I Die - 3 - 2

Verse 2:
Girl, you've got someone you can believe in,
No one can take away what we're feeling.
Our love is strong, it goes on forever,
No one will ever love you better.
And when I'm gone, I'll still be true to you,
The seed of love lives inside of you.
I'll be your angel up in heaven,
And all my love will shine down on you.

# WHAT IF

Words and Music by
**DIANE WARREN**
*Arranged by DAN COATES*

**Moderately**

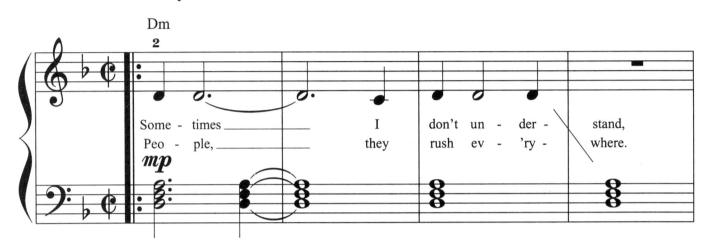

Some - times _____ I don't un - der - stand,
Peo - ple, _____ they rush ev - 'ry - where.

feels like I'm liv - ing in a world gone mad. _____
No time to ev - er take the time to care. _____

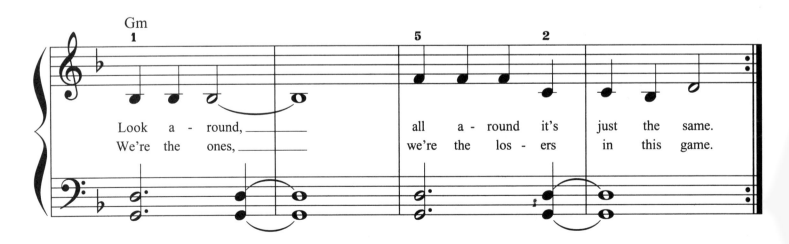

Look a - round, _____ all a - round it's just the same.
We're the ones, _____ we're the los - ers in this game.

What If - 6 - 1

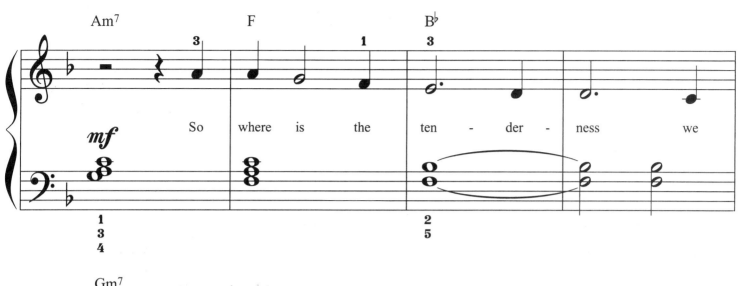

So where is the ten - der - ness we

sac - ri - fice _____ for pro - gress? _____

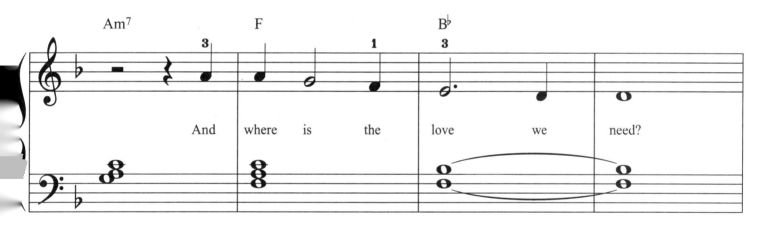

And where is the love we need?

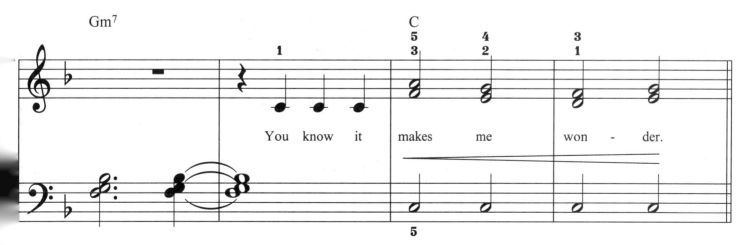

You know it makes me won - der.

What If - 6 - 2

162

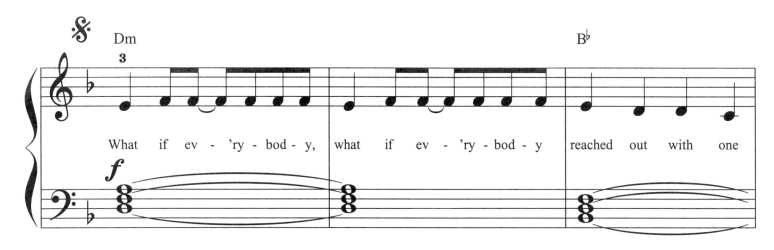

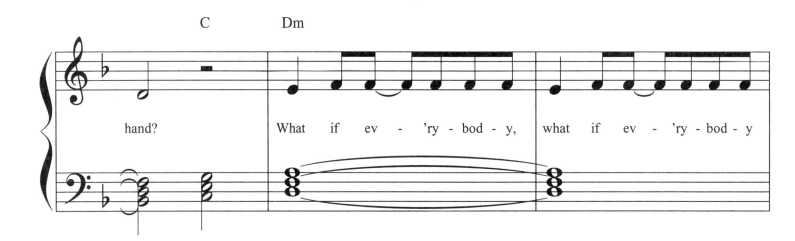

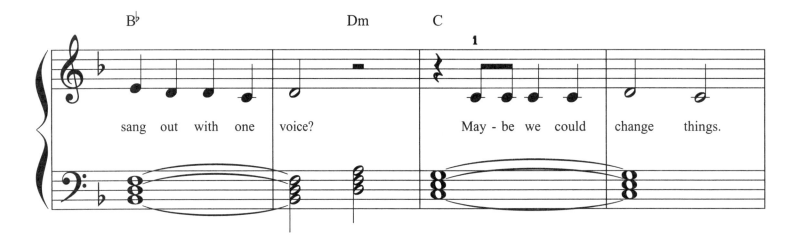

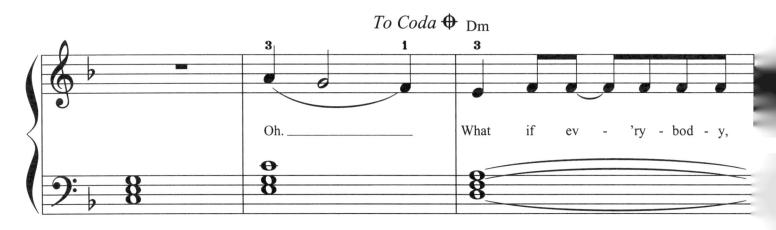

# YOU'RE NOT ALONE

*Arranged by*
*JOHN BRIMHALL*

Words and Music by
TIM KELLETT and
ROBIN TAYLOR-FIRTH

You're Not Alone - 4 - 1

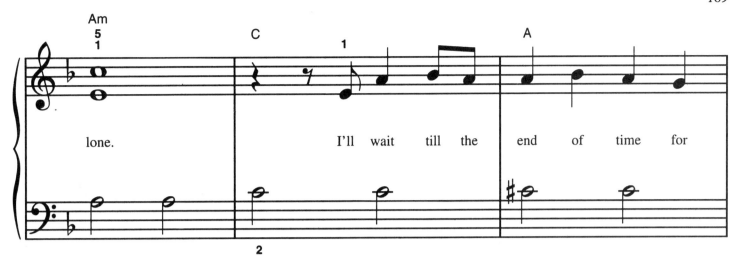

lone.　I'll wait till the　end of time for

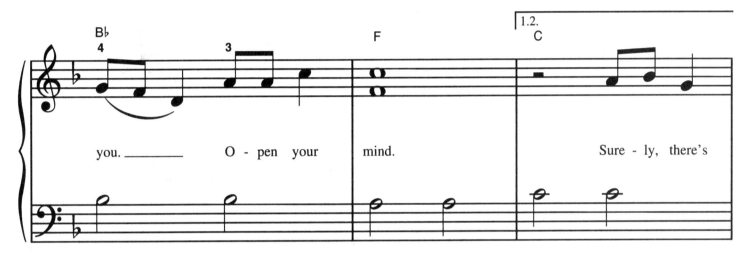

you. _____ O - pen your　mind.　Sure - ly, there's

time to be with me.

*Verse 2:*
It is the distance that makes life a little hard.
Two minds that once were close, now so many miles apart.
I will not falter, though I'll hold on till you're home,
Safely back where you belong, and see how our love has grown.
*(To Chorus:)*

# YOU AND THE MONA LISA

*Arranged by*
*JOHN BRIMHALL*

Words and Music by
SHAWN COLVIN and
JOHN LEVENTHAL

You and the Mona Lisa - 4 - 1

You and the Mona Lisa - 4 - 2

*Verse 2:*
Nothing in particular and everything in between,
This is what you mean to me.
Only you and only me, climbing in the right direction,
On the way to everything.

*Chorus 2:*
We were walking up high,
And no one thought to try.
But I was the one to blame,
And it was just a mirage.
So I hid in the garage
'Til somebody called your name.
*(Intrumental Solo:)*

# WHERE'S THE LOVE

Arranged by
*JOHN BRIMHALL*

Words and Music by
ISAAC HANSON, TAYLOR HANSON, ZACHARY HANSON,
MARK HUDSON and STEVEN SALOVER

Where's the Love - 5 - 1

176

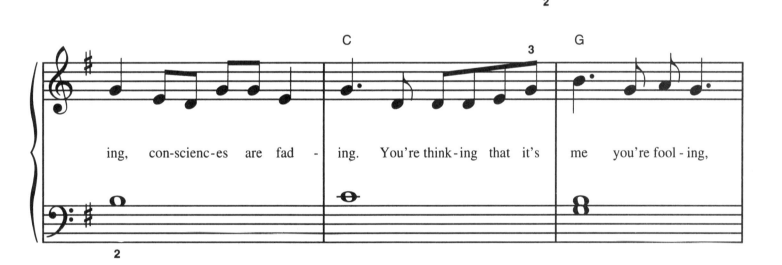

*From the Columbia Pictures Release "YOU LIGHT UP MY LIFE"*

# YOU LIGHT UP MY LIFE

Words and Music by
JOE BROOKS
*Arranged by DAN COATES*

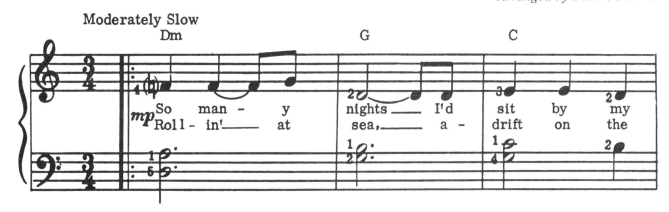

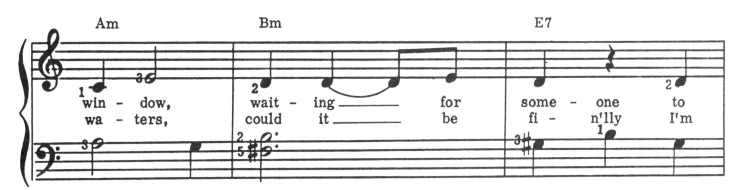

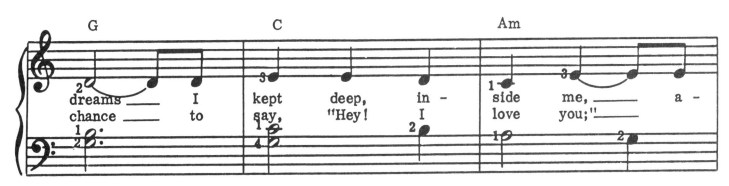

You Light up My Life - 3 - 1

180

You Light up My Life - 3 - 2

You Light up My Life - 3 - 3

# YOU WERE MEANT FOR ME

Words and Music by
JEWEL KILCHER and STEVE POLTZ
*Arranged by DAN COATES*

**Moderate swing feel**

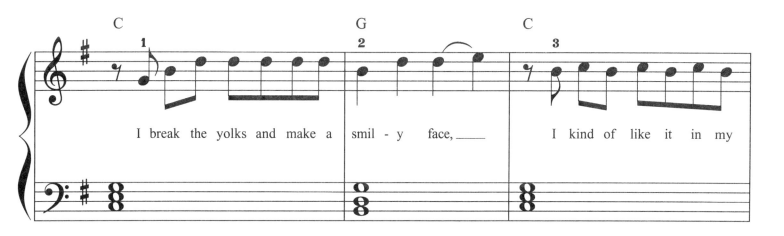

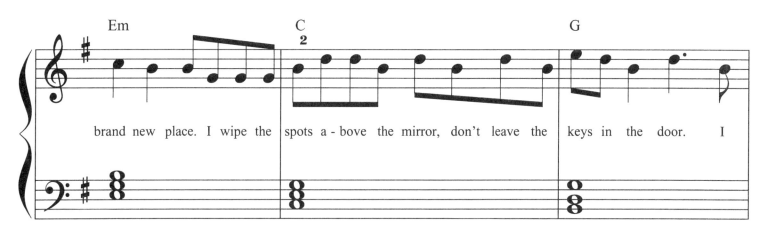

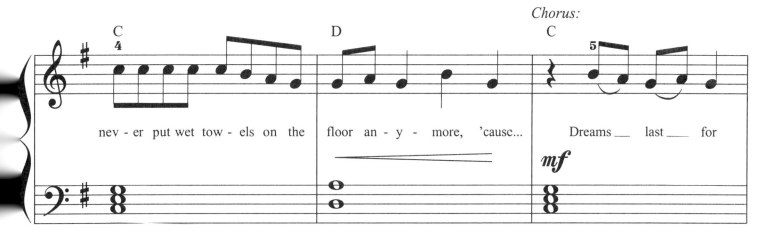

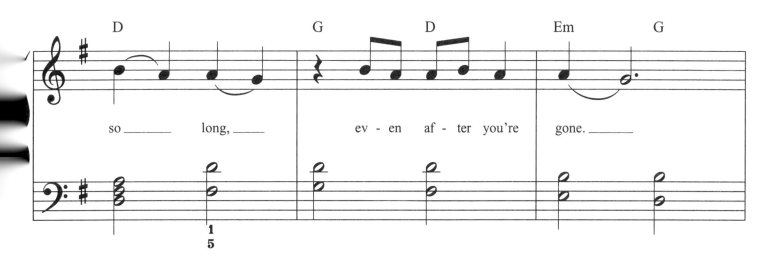

184

You Were Meant for Me - 5 - 3

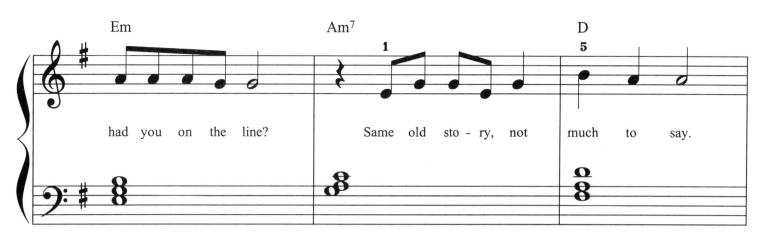

had you on the line? Same old sto - ry, not much to say.

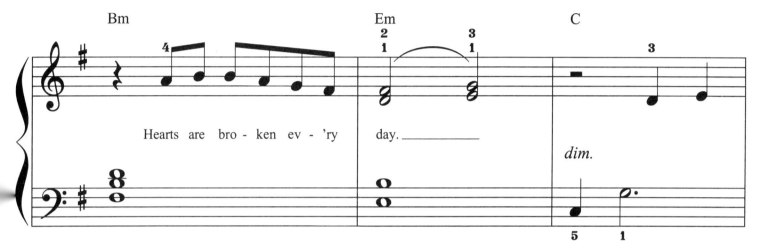

Hearts are bro - ken ev - 'ry day. _____

*dim.*

*D.S.* 𝄋 *al Coda*

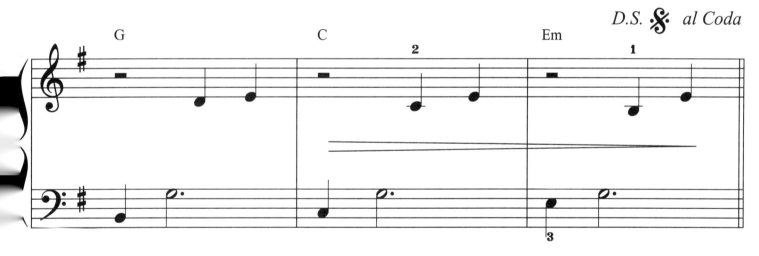

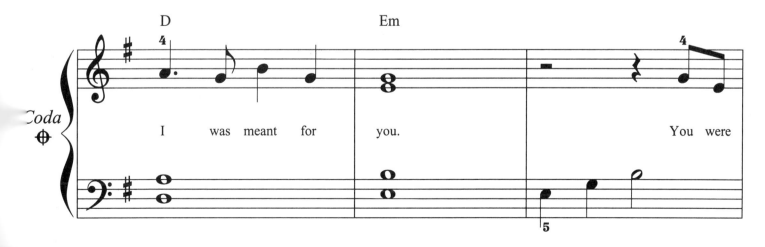

*Coda*

I was meant for you. You were

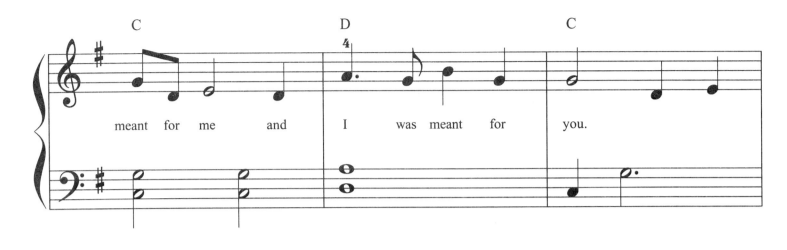

meant for me and I was meant for you.

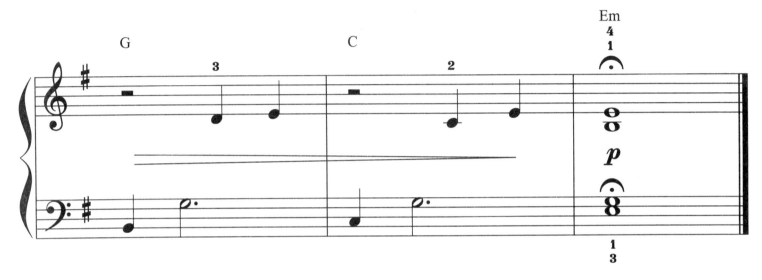

*Verse 2:*
I called my mama, she was out for a walk.
Consoled a cup of coffee, but it didn't wanna talk.
So I picked up a paper, it was more bad news,
More hearts being broken or people being used.
Put on my coat in the pouring rain.
I saw a movie, it just wasn't the same,
'Cause it was happy and I was sad,
And it made me miss you, oh, so bad.
*(To Chorus:)*

*Verse 3:*
I brush my teeth and put the cap back on.
I know you hate it when I leave the light on.
I pick a book up and then I turn the sheets down,
And then I take a breath and a good look around.
Put on my pj's and hop into bed.
I'm half alive but I feel mostly dead.
I try and tell myself it'll be all right,
I just shouldn't think anymore tonight.
*(To Chorus:)*

# Music for Big Note Piano
## from
# Dan Coates

### The Best in Popular Sheet Music
#### (AF9607)

The title says it all! These 25 songs are indeed the best in popular sheet music. Selections include: Angels Among Us • From a Distance • The Greatest Love of All • Have You Ever Really Loved a Woman? • I Swear • I Will Always Love You • Now and Forever • The Rose • Stairway to Heaven • Streets of Philadelphia • Take a Bow and many more.

### Dan Coates Best Big Hits in Big Notes
#### Country Edition
#### (AF9569)

Contains: Angels Among Us (Alabama) • The Dance (Garth Brooks) • Desperado (Clint Black) • I Can Love You Like That (John Michael Montgomery) • I Still Believe in You (Vince Gill) • I Will Always Love You (Dolly Parton) • In This Life (Collin Raye) • The Keeper of the Stars (Tracy Byrd) and more.

### Dan Coates Best Big Hits in Big Notes
#### Movie Edition
#### (AF9566)

Include: Arthur's Theme (Best That You Can Do) *(Arthur)* • Over the Rainbow *(The Wizard of Oz)* • Somewhere in My Memory *(Home Alone)* • Star Wars (Main Theme) *(Star Wars)* • Theme from *Ice Castles* (Through the Eyes of Love) *(Ice Castles)* • You Got It *(Boys on the Side)* and others.

### Dan Coates Best Big Hits in Big Notes
#### Pop Edition
#### (AF9568)

Titles include: From a Distance (Bette Midler) • The Greatest Love of All (Whitney Houston) • Have You Ever Really Loved a Woman? (Bryan Adams) • Save the Best for Last (Venessa Williams) • Stairway to Heaven (Led Zeppelin) • Theme from *New York, New York* (Frank Sinatra) • Tears in Heaven (Eric Clapton) and others.

### Dan Coates Best Big Hits in Big Notes
#### TV Edition
#### (AF9567)

Titles include: Anywhere the Heart Goes ("The Thorn Birds") • Ashokan Farewell ("The Civil War") • Beverly Hills, 90210 (Main Theme) ("Beverly Hills, 90210") • I'll Be There for You ("Friends") • Jeopardy Theme ("Jeopardy") • This Is It! ("The Bugs Bunny Show") and more.

### Dan Coates Big Note Piano Collection
#### (Pop, Country, Movie & TV Hits)
#### (AF9570)

Over 50 of the most popular titles in music today including: Angels Among Us • The Dance • From a Distance • The Greatest Love of All • Have You Ever Really Loved a Woman? • (Everything I Do) I Do It for You • I Swear • I Will Always Love You • I'll Be There for You (Theme from "Friends") • Save the Best for Last • Tears in Heaven and many more.

### Fantastic TV & Movie Songs
#### (AF9532)

Television and movie melodies loved by everyone. Titles include: Ashokan Farewell • Beverly Hills 90210 (Main Theme) • Have You Ever Really Loved a Woman? • I Cross My Heart • I Will Always Love You • The Rose • Theme from *Love Affair* • (I've Had) The Time of My Life • Tiny Toon Adventures Theme Song • Tomorrow.

### The Wizard of Oz
#### (AF9692)

The eye-catching full-color cover — featuring the film's original 50th anniversary artwork — is bound to make this fantastic folio a real collector's item. Titles are: Ding-Dong! The Witch Is Dead • If I Only Had a Brain • The Merry Old Land of Oz • Optimistic Voices • Over the Rainbow • We're Off to See the Wizard and more.

**WARNER BROS. PUBLICATIONS**
15800 N.W. 48th Avenue • Miami, Florida 33014
A Warner Music Group Company